THE SIGNS
AND
INVOLVEMENTS
OF
GOD

THE SIGNS
AND
INVOLVEMENTS
OF
GOD

DON UHM

WinePress WP Publishing

WinePress Publishing (PO Box 428, Enumclaw, WA 98022) functions only as book publisher. As such, the ultimate design, content, editorial accuracy, and views expressed or implied in this work are those of the author.

Unless otherwise noted, all Scriptures are taken from the *Holy Bible, New International Version*®, NIV®. Copyright © 1973, 1978, 1984 by Biblica, Inc.™ Used by permission of Zondervan. All rights reserved worldwide. www.zondervan.com

ISBN 13: 978-1-57921-992-5
ISBN 10: 1-57921-992-6
Library of Congress Catalog Card Number: 2009922519

CONTENTS

PREFACE

We live in a changing world of technological, biological, and mental complexity. The remarkable changes are converging globally into a new computer-culture that is expanding rapidly. We are entering a hi-tech age that is unique to mankind. The rapid technological changes, from manual to digital, with tremendous scientific improvements, have led us to embrace a materialistic worldview.

Simultaneously the world is on the verge of the greatest crisis among conflicting economic, political, cultural, moral, energy-intensive, environmental, and religious interests in human history. We also face tremendous challenges from natural disasters all over the world: Hurricanes, tsunamis, bird flu, earthquakes, and terrorism—a mixture of political and religious hatred.

Despite this rapidly changing period, we still need to pursue solutions to these difficult problems. Without such solutions, we cannot live meaningful lives, our values will be impacted negatively, and our goals will not be as lofty. Thankfully, solutions do exist. History has a meaning and a direction.

That simple statement leads to the many questions we'll explore in this book: What is history? Where do we come from? Why do we exist? Who are we? Where are we going? Did the God of the Bible create the universe and everything in it? Is the Bible reliable as the true Word of God? Will there be an end to history?

ACKNOWLEDGMENTS

First, I dedicate this book to my Lord, Jesus Christ.

A number of people contributed to my preparation of this book in various ways, stimulating my thinking by contributing ideas and information. I particularly want to thank my wife Mary, Karen Lee, and my church members.

Some have influenced my thinking and writing on matters discussed in this book, and I owe them a debt of gratitude, especially Susan Osborn and Lee Warren, who reviewed this manuscript and gave me great advice. Thanks also to my two daughters, Dr. Grace Park, who gave me a number of good suggestions, and Dr. Helen Choi, who had a great concern for this book.

INTRODUCTION

The Bible teaches clearly that God created space, time, and life, as well as matter and energy. Everything God created has a systematic order to it. This biblical view of creation stands up when compared to other historical records and archaeological findings. Therefore, we must not fear the findings of evolutionists.

In fact, we are obliged to consider the contribution of all fields of study if we want to do justice to the truth. The basis of this book, however, is rooted in the belief that God is the source of all creation. The book deals with the origin of everything and its related matters by examining the various evidences to prove the truth of their reliabilities and our subsequent human responsibility.

CHAPTER ONE

THE AWE AND WONDER

When we gaze at the clear night sky after rain, countless stars cause us to raise profound questions about the origin of the universe—especially the motions of the planets in the solar system that revolve around the sun in elliptical orbits. How and why do they have those motions? I definitely believe what scientists say: There must be complex rules or laws governing the world and those rules have been working on earth and in our solar system since it came into existence.

We breathe in oxygen and let out carbon dioxide, and it is theoretically feasible that carbon dioxide will fill up the earth and no one will survive. But this has never happened and mankind has never run out of oxygen because of the cycles that keep the earth's ecosystems in balance. We are surrounded by well-prepared, beautiful symmetry. Where did all of this come from? And what is the meaning of it all? In order for us to get the right answers to these questions, we need to know the definition of a word I'm going to refer to often. The word is *system*.

Generally, a system is defined as a group of independent but inter-related elements that make up a unified and consistent whole. By definition, if the components of a system are divided, or working against one another, they really are not part of a system at all. The systems of the universe, or the order of things, consist of meaning and purpose—not randomness. Inherently, we know this to be true.

In order to clean dirty clothes, man invented the washing machine. The machine is equipped with many options, including a setting for such things as the perceived dirt level, the fabric type, and the load size. Even though the machine has many options, they all work together to produce clean clothes.

Trees need dirt, wind, nutrition, water, sunlight, oxygen, and nitrogen for their survival, each having a function that works toward the survival of the tree. Even man himself is a type of a system. We have a brain, heart, lungs, kidneys, nerves, hands, feet, bones, joints, and muscles, all of which are part of our biological makeup, or system.

All of us have profound connections to this planet. As such, all the matter around us is related to each other for a specific purpose. No one can deny that the systems and their rules are fundamental and basic foundations and realities in our lives. Their existences are already known, issued, and proven, not only by many individuals but also social common sense.

However, most people have not paid attention to these profound systems. Professor and author Howard A. Snyder says, "All things are connected, not only by the human mind, but also more deeply, through an inbuilt or inherent order that is really there."[1] Neil Broom, a professor in the department of chemical and materials engineering at Auckland in New Zealand, clearly shows us an example of the existence of systems and rules: "The living cell operates in principle just like any man-made mechanical system with all the appearances of having been constructed according to principles of engineering design."[2]

---

[1] Howard. A Snyder, *Earthcurrents: The Struggle for the World's Soul* (Nashville: Abingdon Press, 1995), p. 264.
[2] Neil Broom, *How Blind Is the Watchmaker* (Downers Grove: InterVarsity Press. 2nd. Edition, 2001), pp. 46–47.

Systems have order and the order allows us to live peacefully on earth. What is, then, the definition of order? It is usually defined as a maintaining factor, coherent pattern, and an expression of profound natural law in the system, and its function is a connective and directive faculty within system networks toward a certain goal. Every system, therefore, functions properly. But their existence and function is mysterious from the scientific perspective. Order makes systems work normally, and systems work simultaneously with order. If you don't have order, you don't have a system. If you don't have a system you don't have order.

But when you do have order, you find beauty, wonder, and harmony. William Demski, a mathematician and philosopher, says this about the existence of order: "For nature to be an object of inquiry for the scientist, nature must have an order which the scientist can grasp. If nature were totally without form and order, no science would be possible."[3]

We see this order everywhere, from social, political, biological, cosmological, and ecological structures, to our human body. And of course, we see it every time the earth revolves around the sun. Howard Snyder says, "We see then that the universe, at least as a physical place, is marked by both order and surprise."[4]

The existence of order in the various systems of the universe leads us to question how and where this purposeful order came from. Does this order come from "accidental chance"? Is it even possible for order to create and sustain itself? We don't believe that automobiles, airplanes, cell phones, navigation devices, DVD players, or any other form of technology is self-creating or self-sustaining. We know they absolutely require a higher level of creation and a built in process to work properly.

---

[3] William A. Demski, *Intelligent Design* (Downers Grove: InterVarsity Press, 1999), p. 98.
[4] Howard A. Snyder, *Earthcurrents*, p. 252.

Why is it any different with the universe? The complexity of order in the universe points to a Creator who made all things (Gen. 1:1–31; Eccl. 3:1–8; 2 Kings 20:1; Ps. 94:9; Ps. 104:2–9; Job 9:6–12; 14:5; 26:7, 10; 38:4–7) and holds all things together (Ps. 136:5; 148:3–5). We can conclude that the universe and all living things must have systems that consist of a remarkably precise order and condition, providing proper and necessary components, all the extremely exquisite constants and precisions, and a higher level of process and control.

We can get more detailed facts through two different areas— cosmology and biology.

From the Cosmos: What Is Cosmology?

Cosmology is the study of tracing the harmoniously and systematically well-organized physical universe—the solar system, galaxy, etc.—and its origin, structure, and development. Webster's dictionary defines it as the totality of all things that exist.[5] The universe consists of a multiplicity of objects and complex systems. Paul Davies, a mathematical physicist, clearly defines the universe as undeniably complex, but its complexity is of an organized variety.[6] In order for people and other organisms to live, well-organized and interrelated conditions with the right elements must exist. In order for the material universe to keep a harmonious balance, there should also be numerous natural laws in action. Scientists find more and more of these natural laws on a regular basis. Physicist Hugh Ross states, "Everything about the universe tends toward man, toward making life possible and sustaining it."[7]

---

[5] *Webster's Dictionary of the English Language Unabridged-Encyclopedia Edition* (New York: Publishers International Press).
[6] Paul Davies, *The Unreasonable Effectiveness of Science in "Evidence of Purpose"* edited by John Marks Templeton (New York: Continumm, 1994), p. 45.
[7] Hugh Ross, *The Fingerprint of God* (Orange, CA: Promise Publishing Co. 1989), p. 120.

Here are some strong supporting evidences of a well-ordered creation:

- Stars have good balance in the force of gravity between them that allows for their harmonious stability.
- The distance between the stars leads to the stability of orbits.[8]
- The sun and earth have the necessary distance between them for their harmonious stability.
- This distance between the sun and the earth allows for stability for living organisms on earth.
- The earth constantly revolves around the sun, which is conducive for desirable temperatures and the changes of the seasons.
- The earth's rotation leads to the change of day and night.
- The earth is tipped at 23.5 degrees with respect to the plane of revolution around the sun, which leads to climates that are conducive for human existence.
- Planets continually rotate around the sun.
- There is constant proper gravitational interaction with the moon that allows for an effective earthly ocean tide.
- The necessary oxygen quantity in the earth's atmosphere is sufficient for living organisms.[9]
- There are constant rainy seasons on earth that benefit all kinds of life.
- The earth consists of necessary gas levels such as oxygen, nitrogen, hydrogen, carbon dioxide, and ozone for people and other living organisms.
- There is unchanging proper salty water of the sea for oceanic organisms.
- There are constant air currents on the earth.

---

[8] Ibid., p.127.
[9] Ibid., p. 131.

Our Human Bodies

Our bodies consist of many different organs that are inter-related and interdependent, all of which makes up a highly complex system. Geoffrey Simmons, a medical doctor, says, "The formation of each cell and every function thereof follows a blueprint that is drawn up at the union of the egg and sperm."[10] Cell systems must be programmed by design. Consider the way the body continually goes through the process of renewal, recycle, protection, and adjustment.

The Digestive System

Food flows down the gastrointestinal tract and is absorbed through the walls of the small intestine, into the bloodstream, through the liver—extracting nutrients from food and delivering them to every cell in the body, thereby maintaining the health of the whole body.

The Immune System

The immune system has two main elements with white blood cells and antibodies circulating in the blood with the antigen-antibody reaction forming the basis for this immunity.

When a harmful foreign substance—such as viruses, bacterium, funguses, or parasites—invades the body, a specific antibody produced in the body attacks the foreign harmful substance. Even when we get sick, the produced antibody may either destroy the antigen directly or white cells can swallow up the foreign intruder by built-in defense mechanisms.

The Breathing System

When we run or go up into the high altitude of the mountains, we cannot breathe normally because physiological changes take

---

[10] Geoffrey Simmons, *What Darwin Didn't Know* (Eugene, OR: Harvest House Publishers, 2004), p. 53.

place in our body. But after our panting mechanism kicks in to make adjustments, we eventually return to a normal breathing pattern. And we adjust to the new situation or climate.

The Skin System

We know that our skin is an organ designed to protect us. Geoffrey Simmons says that our skin is the largest and heaviest organ and weighs six to ten pounds; in the average adult it covers an area of twenty-two square feet.[11] Our skin is a highly complex system that covers the entire body with lots of functioning factors including flexes, folds, and crinkles around joints. It has varying textures like hardness, softness, and roughness. It also recognizes information about our environment, monitors the variety of stimuli in wind, and changes in pressure and temperature. But among the many functional tasks of skin, Paul Brand emphasizes that the "skin's most crucial contribution might opt for waterproofing."[12] Sixty percent of the body consists of fluids, and these would soon evaporate without the moist, sheltered world provided by skin. Without skin, a warm bath would kill; fluids would rush in like water over a flooded spillway, swelling the body with liquid, diluting the blood, and waterlogging the lungs. The skin's tight barrier of shingled cells fends off such disasters.[13] Furthermore, skin is thickest where we need more protection, and despite the constant turnover of cells and sloughing of skin, everyone's exterior remains the same.[14]

---

[11] Ibid., p. 151.

[12] Philip Yancy and Paul Brand, *Fearfully and Wonderfully Made* (Grand Rapids: Zondervan, 1980), p. 151.

[13] Ibid., p. 151.

[14] Simmons, *What Darwin Didn't Know*, p. 163.

The Muscular System

Our muscles are remarkable organs. We have more than six hundred different muscle groups.[15] They help us move, change shape, and lift heavy objects. For instance, some muscles contribute to hand movements, and some, barely an inch long, allow for a spectrum of subtle expression in the face. The diaphragm controls coughing, breathing, sneezing, and laughing, and thigh muscles equip the body for a lifetime of walking. Without muscles, bones would collapse in a heap, joints would slip apart, and movement would cease.[16] Our muscle systems are also interrelated and interdependent with all kinds of other organs, such as nerves, skin, arteries, and veins for harmonious motion and desirable health.

How could all of these systems that are so beautifully and wonderfully knit together, be accidental? Well-organized systems require a higher level of precise process and design: An accidental chance cannot survive. Therefore when we face the issue of what is known about all the mechanisms for the origin of living systems, we must confess that these are from the Creator God. Specifically, modern science impacts our understanding of the Creator God in a number of ways upon. He created with a purpose so that we humans can also participate, and He sustains the world throughout time and space. In particular, the discovery of purpose in the creative activity of God can become the source of meaning in life.

---

[15] Ibid., p. 221.

[16] Philip Yancey and Paul Brand, *Fearfully and Wonderfully Made*, pp. 163–164.

CHAPTER TWO

THE SIGNS AND INVOLVEMENTS OF GOD

As long as people have existed, their curiosity—an aspect of their ability to think and to question the origin of everything—has driven them to search both their own origin and origins of other things. How did these things come to be what they are today? Are they by-products of an accidental chance, or created by a super intelligent Creator, who is self-existent?

Creationists have the simple and clear answer. It is documented in the Bible, which describes God as the Creator, who made everything "out of nothing." The existence of things, living and non-living, and above all, mankind, remain the best historical record of evidence for creationism. Our belief in creation enables us to see the universe and life forms as dependents upon God's sustaining power, wisdom, and activity. On this basis, we confirm that we are not the end products of meaningless processes in an impersonal world, but we are created in the image of a personal, loving God. Specifically, we were commissioned to take dominion over the created world as the Creator's earthly agent (Gen. 1:28).

History is a way of explaining the progression of God's plan through humanity toward an ultimate destination. On this basis, we must assume the starting point of history began with the creative act of a Creator. Arthur F. Glasser says that "history means movement."[1] We must look beneath the surface of external events to try to find significant meaning. In the grand scale, history is a progressive movement toward the Creator's ultimate destination; not by accidental movement without any goal. Accordingly, history gives us the final direction of the will of God. Howard A. Snyder defines it clearly by saying that history is not "haphazard happenstance" and has an "external" as well as "internal" meaning.[2] James W. Sire explains that "history is linear, a meaningful sequence of events leading to the fulfillment of God's purpose for humanity, and history itself is a form of revelation and is the record of the involvement and concern of God in human events (especially as localized in the Jewish people)."[3]

The apostle Paul declared the indivisible connection between the historical factual basis of God's involvement in our world and the Christian faith as follows: "If it is preached that Christ has been raised from the dead, how can some of you say that there is no resurrection of the dead? And if Christ has not been raised, our preaching is useless and so is your faith."[4]

In addition, such special events as the birth, death, and resurrection of Jesus Christ, the Son of God, which took place in the historical world in space and time, are important because they provide Christians with an absolute foundation of faith, disclosing the important meaning and direction of history. Particularly, the primary sources of these events are the testimonies of the disciples of Jesus Christ on His deity and historicity as eyewitnesses.

---

[1] Arthur F. Glasser, *The Word Among Us,* edited by Dean S. Gilland (Word Publishing, 1989), p. 34.
[2] Howard A. Snyder, *Earthcurrents: The Struggle for the World's Soul,* p. 264.
[3] James W. Sire, *The Universe Next Door,* (Downers Grove: InterVarsity Press, 3rd ed.), pp. 36–37.
[4] 1 Corinthians 15:12–14, *NIV Bible.*

God is not only Lord over the whole of history, but He continues to govern and rule in the affairs of man based upon his eternal plan and will. John Bright, a theologian and author, says, "History must have a future, a destination."[5] Christ, as the Son of God, visibly entered our human history in order to manifest and fulfill God's redemptive plan for mankind. The peak of history was embodied in the historical virgin birth, sacrificial redemptive death on the cross, and resurrection of Jesus Christ. If history were merely an accidental chance, there would be no basis for hope. For history to have significant meaning, it must have the possibility of hope and be headed toward a certain goal. And what more hope can be found, but in that of the empty tomb?

---

[5] John Bright, *The Kingdom of God*, (New York: Abingdon-Cokesbury, 1953), p. 30.

CHAPTER THREE

THE CHARACTERISTICS OF HUMANITY

God, in His infinite love for us, gave man commandments to follow and the free will to decide whether we will do so.

"The LORD will establish you as a people holy to himself, as he has sworn to you, if you keep the commandments of the LORD your God and walk in his ways" (Deut. 28:9).

Of course, we can never earn God's favor, even by exercising our free will in favor of walking in the ways of the Lord. But by virtue of the fact that God cares enough about us to give us free will is yet more evidence that God loves us.

The exercise of free will is implied throughout the Bible (Exod. 20:1–17; Ps. 103:11; Matt. 22:37–40; Luke 11:9). It should be noted that only man has two components—the physical and the spiritual. Man's spirituality means that we have an attribution of seeking the Creator, God. Animals do what they were designed to do. They don't struggle with moral dilemmas. They simply react instinctively. And while that may seem to be the ultimate form of freedom, in reality, nothing brings freedom like willfully obeying the commands of God.

Imagine going skiing and deciding that you would rather not use skis to make your way down the mountain because you find them too restrictive. You feel completely free because you are doing things your way; but that changes when you step onto the slope. You end up with a face full of snow while skiers go flying by you. At that point, you would probably change your mind about how restrictive skis appear to be, and you would decide to put on a pair so you could experience the mountain the way it was intended to be enjoyed. So it is with God's law.

If we do not have free will and spirituality, then we are no different from animals that are bound by their instincts. God wants us to obey His laws because they enhance personal relationships, they keep social order, they improve our lives, and of course, in doing so, we show Him by will how much we love Him.

Free will is a prerequisite for spiritual beings, but it is not desirable to be exercised beyond the spiritual boundaries God has set in place. If we do go beyond the boundaries, then consequences will follow.

What about organisms? Are they antonymous? I will grant that they do have an element of renewal and recyclability while maintaining the integrity of their overall structures. All living things tend to establish their heights, sizes, colors, and textures to a certain degree according to internal principles that are interdependent on environmental and circumstantial influences.

The system of self-formation exhibits a certain degree of autonomy with internal pliability and flexibility and with a number of characteristic and creative properties. However, its function is determined by productive relations and by given purposes. This does not mean that all living systems are separated from their external and circumstantial environment. On the contrary, they interact with it continually, obtaining the necessary substances from environmental context, but this interaction does not ultimately determine their survival. Instead, their survival depends upon their abilities given to them by a Creator.

No matter whether we are talking about people or angels or other living organisms, a harmonious relationship with God is based upon exercising free will within the boundaries that God has set. God does not want to control the will of humans or angels. Instead He wants us to choose to follow Him.

CHAPTER FOUR

THE ORIGIN OF SATAN AND HIS POSITION AT THE JUDGMENT

Throughout human history, people have recognized, and in many cases perpetrated, evil in this world. Indeed, evil was passed on to us with tremendous impact upon our lives in many ways. It gives us disorderly impulses and desires such as pain and suffering. The puzzling and painful problem of evil often causes us to question God. Where can we find the source of information about Satan? Why does God allow evil to happen? Why doesn't He seem to show up when we believe He should? And if God isn't the source of evil, then why does it appear to reign so often? The Bible is the only authoritative source of information about Satan, who is spoken of directly over two hundred times.

God created angels without physical or material bodies, as special agents, who possess great knowledge and power that are derived from God. They remain dependent on His favorable will to exercise it. But they are not omniscient (2 Pet. 2:11), and they are restricted to exercising their free will within the limits of His spiritual system and permission. How, then, did evil come into existence?

The books of Jude (6) and Job (1:12; 2:6) give us a direct clue. They describe Satan's fall. But before we talk about that any further, we need to be clear in saying that all created entities are under God's authority. If any violation of God's law (cause) occurs, then serious consequences (effect) will follow. Accordingly, the origin of evil was a direct result of cause and effect. When we love others (cause), others will love us (effect); when we hate others (cause), they will hate us (effect). Our Creator made the universe and all living things (cause), and they continue to exist (effect). If we hit a concrete wall, our hands get hurt.

L.S. Chafer defines "evil" and "sin" as follows: "Evil refers to what, though latent and not expressed, is conceivable as the opposite of what is good. Sin is what is concrete and actively opposed to the character of God."[1] As such, angels must be in compliance with God's law in order to live holy and harmoniously. According to the Bible, there was a legion of angels who used to belong to the good angels. Their leader was Lucifer, who was a beautiful, intelligent creature of God and of the highest order of angels, an archangel. Pride got the best of him and he fell from God's grace (Isa. 14:12–15; Ezek. 28:12–17; Jude 6).

Satan and his followers lost their privilege of serving God, and were referred to as devils and evil spirits with different names (Deut. 32:17; Job 1:6; Gen. 3:1–6; Mark 1:23; 1 Cor. 10:20–21; 2 Cor. 11:3; 1 Tim. 4:1). They were cast out of the heavenly realms and no longer hold their positions as servants of God (Luke 10:18; Jude 6).

The inhabited earth is clearly designated by the word "cosmos" (Rom. 1:8) in the Bible. That is why Satan is called both the god of this age (2 Cor. 4:4), the prince of this world (John 12:31), and the "prince of the power of the air" (Eph. 2:2). The Bible teaches that Satan, as a fallen angel, has authority over the

---

[1] Chafer, *Systematic Theology*, vol. p. 360.

cosmos. Even Jesus Christ called Satan the ruler of the world (John 12:31, 16:11). The earth is Satan's playground. He is gifted with high intelligence (Gen. 3) and great power, unlike people (Matt. 4:1–10; Luke 10:18; Rom. 16:20; Rev. 12:7).

Soon after he violated God's law, Satan and his group of fallen angels were bound with everlasting chains and are held until the great Day of Judgment (Jude 6). However, their disobedience cannot upset the stability of the cosmos. God will prevail. Satan and his followers will not descend to hell until Christ casts them into the Lake of Fire after their final rebellion at the end of the Millennium (Rev. 20:1–15).

CHAPTER FIVE

SATAN'S GOAL

Satan—often referred to as principalities, powers, the prince of the air, the prince of this darkness, and spiritual hosts of wickedness in high places—began to seriously organize his empire in this world after his fall. His world probably is above and around the earth, and he tries to oppose God's authority and to destroy His spiritual system and its rule (Eph. 2:2; 6:12). His violation of God's spiritual system with a group of angels brought contamination to this world. He uses evil weapons such as: impurity, debauchery, idolatry, fits of rage, selfish ambition, immorality, witchcraft, dissensions, factions, drunkenness, orgies, lies, slander, brutality, treacherousness, abusiveness, vanity, and a denial of the power of God. All such characteristics are commonly exhibited among humans.

In order to achieve his goal, Satan has been trying to tempt people to violate God's law by using his wicked weapons with false ideas. His power is recognizable in many aspects of today's modern world, and much strange phenomena in people's actions today simply cannot be accounted for unless we recognize the evil behind it.

Evil is seen not only as the force behind the brutal nature of modern crime, but also behind the more subtle and penetrative spirit of this age, which motivates people to do evil in countless ways.

The following agendas are the main ingredients of Satan's strategy:

- Let people fundamentally deny the existence of God.
- Let people believe they are autonomous and unaccountable to God.
- Let people believe that moral absolutes do not exist.
- Let people believe that all religions are the pathway to heaven.
- Let people think they are more important than anyone or anything else.
- Let people place a higher priority on their kingdom than on God's kingdom.
- Let people focus on the now rather than on eternal life.

CHAPTER SIX

THE MASTERPIECE OF GOD

The preceding chapters give us convincing facts about the origin of the universe, life, angels, God's law, and evil. Now we will focus on the most valuable masterpiece of God: humans, both male and female. The Bible says that only humans are made in the image and likeness of God (Gen. 1:27). We are the crown of creation. People are unique because being created in the "image of God" means that we are expected to live on spiritual and moral grounds, not instinct only.

James W. Sire summarizes the nature of human beings, by saying that like God, we have personality, self-transcendence, intelligence (the capacity for reason and knowledge), morality (the capacity for recognizing and understanding good and evil), social capacity (our characteristic and fundamental desire and need for human companionship) and creativity (the ability to imagine new things or to endow old things with human significance).[1] Similarly, accredited theologian, Wayne Grudem, states that human beings in many ways represent the God of creation.[2] Because we reflect

---

[1] James W. Sire, *The Universe Next Door* (Downers Grove: InterVarsity Press, 1997 3rd ed.), p. 29.
[2] Wayne Grudem, *Systematic Theology*, p. 443.

the Creator, we are expected to comply within His spiritual rules and carry out His purpose on earth.

We must fully understand that the dignity and value of people is from God. We are divine vessels for divine grace and for conformity to God's image. In order to be children of God in His eternal plan, we must know who we are. This question of who we are has been discussed as a fundamental and principal issue for nearly as long as man has been in existence. Philosophers in ancient Greek times believed people were primarily a spirit and a body and that the body is of a lower order of reality. Materialists believe that humans are simply a product of nature; therefore a person is treated only as a part of the material substance of society, not as an important and valuable individual. But the biblical perspective proclaims that people were created in the image of God.

People are equipped with the ineradicable faculties of the free will, intelligence, morality, and emotion. We are also task-oriented beings who need structure. God created us with a spirit, a soul, and a body (1 Thess. 5:23). In contrast to the material part of people, the immaterial part of a person is not said to be created but was breathed out by God. On the other hand, God created angels as immaterial beings with a material body. They were not made from a preexisting entity (Ezek. 28:15). The fact that the immaterial nature of people was not created seems to imply that God imparted something of His own nature into them (Gen. 1:27). God has distinguished the spirit of a person from their soul (Gen. 2:7) and placed these in a created earthen body.

In general, the soul seems to relate primarily to psychological or natural experiences. The spirit, by contrast, seems to relate more to religious experiences. The physical body comes into contact with the material world. Our soul comprises the intellect to help us find all kinds of mysteries hidden in the present state of existence to a certain degree and the emotion to proceed from our senses for abundant life. In addition, the soul reveals our personality.

If our human spirit complies with God's law, then our soul rules over our own passions as desired by God, and we can rule over the earth by carrying out divine plans as representatives of God for His glory. As a consequence, we will receive great peace and establish a harmonious relationship with God. For this reason, the richly royal life was given to us to carry out His purpose as agents of God on earth. In this sense we are God's masterpiece. However, in order for us to carry out our mission, we must remain faithful to God. The Bible puts it this way:

> Then God said, let us make man in our image, in our likeness, and let them rule over the fish of the sea and birds of the air, over all the earth . . . be fruitful and increase in number and subdue it.
> —Genesis 1:28

> Therefore go and make disciples of all nations, baptizing them in the name of the Father and of the Son and of the Holy Spirit, and teaching them to obey everything I have commanded you.
> —Matthew 28:19

> Yet to all who received Him, to those who believed in His name, He gave the right to become children of God.
> —John 1:12

> As a result, he does not to live the rest of his earthly life for evil human desires, but rather for the will of God.
> —1 Peter 4:2

CHAPTER SEVEN

SATAN'S ATTACK

S atan collected angelic beings as his followers, who too became fallen angels. He readied himself to attack the first man and woman with his rebellious and wicked plans. Adam and Eve's sin in the garden was the beginning of the ills and sorrows that Satan helped to instigate. He continued to work through his fallen angels, humans, or cosmic forces of nature to bring to pass his evil plans. Today, he continues his attempts to turn people away from God by promoting such things as: the importance of our ego; temptation to participate in idol worship (Lev. 17:7; Deut. 32:17; Ps. 106:36–38); false teachings; and by causing people to worship Satan himself (Rev. 13:1–18).

Adam and Eve were innocent and pure when they were created. God put them on earth in fertile and beautiful surroundings. Furthermore, they had the great privilege of enjoying their relationship with God. God clearly delineated various rules, which consisted of "to dos" and only one "not to do." These served as sign posts for continued blessings and as a safety measure from the attacking force of Satan. He gave them dominion over the earth with one rule: They were not to eat of the tree of the knowledge of good and evil. They were also given a list of things to do in order to maintain the garden.

Adam was "to till and to keep or guard" the garden. This shows us there must have been a dangerous force present that made such a "guarding" necessary. The serpent said, "Did God really say, you must not eat from any tree in the garden. You will not surely die. For God knows that when you eat of it your eyes will be opened, and you will be like God" (Gen. 3:1–5). This proves the inference as a fact.

God told them what the consequences would be if they chose to disobey Him: "for when you eat of it you will surely die" (Gen. 2:17). God designed a world where all peoples are destined to live "under" His law. The Bible repeatedly carries this warning: "A man reaps what he sows" (Gal. 6:7).

If a man has a job, he must obey the rules of the company he works for, and if he works hard he will get paid accordingly. If he sows laziness at work, he will reap pennilessness. He must live with the results.

One day, Satan appeared in the form of a serpent as a tempting agent in front of Eve. He approached her with a question and convinced her to break the only rule God had given to her and her husband. That one sin was passed on to all of humanity, and Satan has been tempting mankind ever since.

Satan cannot be seen with our physical eyes, and is essentially and irretrievably an evil, malevolent creature. He is against God because he lost his position in heaven. His prime motive is to destroy what God loves or creates. Since God loves people more than anything else, Satan wishes to hurt and destroy us. Consequently, when anyone becomes a faithful believer, Satan begins a constant warfare with him or her.

Evil aspired to a position of equality with God. Satan's challenge seems to have been most specifically with the incarnate Jesus Christ. However, this conflict will continue until Satan is cast into the lake of fire forever at the end of this age. The Bible states that this timeframe is known only by God and will end at judgment day (Acts 1:7; Matt. 24:32–33; 2 Tim. 3:1–5; Rev. 20:1–10).

CHAPTER EIGHT

THE MISUSE OF FREE WILL

When Adam and Eve sinned, they ran away from the presence of God. They lost their spiritual privilege of walking closely with Him. In addition, they faced the death of spirit, soul, and body. As a by-product, their line of access to the life-giving God was broken. Their misuse of free will took only a moment, but the consequences are still being felt by their descendents. Furthermore, their genuine characteristics (such as their decision-making process and morality) became terribly warped and damaged. It is similar to a damaged nerve that cannot receive the brain's signals. The body is unable to receive the proper signals, and therefore unable to function properly.

The current presence of evil and sinful practices within humanity stems from the originators' (Adam and Eve) misuse of their free will. Sin is an outcome of the violation of God's rules; therefore sin is manifested in the nature of all humans. Millard J. Erickson, a theologian, explains the root of sin by asserting that "all of us begin life with a natural tendency to sin, and the Bible tells us that with the fall, man's first sin, a radical change took place in the universe."[1] As a result, mankind still experiences spiritual alienation from God, ruin of the soul, physical death, evil thoughts, rejection of God, idolatry, impurity, theft, murder, lying, false witnesses, adultery, greed, malice, deceit, slanderers, arrogance, folly, hatred, brutality, factions, pleasure seekers, boasters, abusiveness, pleasure seekers, and the like (Mark 7:20–22; Gal. 5:19–20; James 3:14; 2 Tim. 3:1–5).

In essence, humanity has experienced a type of earthquake since the first sin. When a high-rise is severely shaken by a strong earthquake of over ten degrees of seismic intensity, its effect on the structure and community is quite evident. Similarly, people have been captive to past errors and will continue to be affected positively and negatively by their use of free will.

---

[1] Milliard J. Erickson, *Christian Theology*, p. 428.

CHAPTER NINE

GROWING CONFLICTS

God's faithfulness to His people shows how closely He is involved in human history. His grace and blessings, and judgments and redemption continue to this day, depending upon how faithful God's people are to follow His commands. The Bible clearly illustrates these promises and punishments as conditions of people's spiritual attitudes and obedience to God.

God commanded Abraham, a common man described in Genesis 12:1–3, to leave the city of Ur and set out for the new land. Willingly, Abraham complied, as God's purpose for him and mankind was to restore His people by setting them apart from the morally polluted world. As a result Abraham and his family were blessed.

While Abraham was greatly blessed, if we examine the existence of his descendents as a nation, it is quite evident they suffered great hardship as consequences for not adhering to God's spiritual laws. This started when God's people were held captive in Egypt for a period of 430 years. When they were freed and traveled to the Promised Land, they turned to idol worship and faced seventy more years in captivity, this time in Babylonia, just as Jeremiah prophesied (606–536 B.C.).

Historical accounts reveal that Abraham's descendents could have taken the opportunity to reap great blessings. But they failed to answer God's call and adhere to His expectations, which again led to great tragedy. The descendents lost their freedom and became subjected to the Roman Empire.

CHAPTER TEN

NEW LIGHT FOR FALLEN PEOPLE

On the heels of the spiritual turmoil, Jesus Christ entered this world through the promised virgin birth. But the descendants of Abraham ignored and rejected this historically factual event. They weren't the only ones. Many people today have a hard time believing that a man was born of a virgin. Our human knowledge is too incomplete to deny the existence and intelligent power of an almighty Creator. Jesus Christ, the One whom they had waited for, came into human history by God's miraculous way in order to restore and save all who call upon His name.

Christ came to this world as both man and God through virgin birth. Many get bogged down by this and use it as a reason not to believe in Jesus or His purpose for existence and resurrection. In consideration of all of modern technology and scientific advances, could this possibility be so absurd or foreign? Medical studies reveal scientists' ability to clone; cellular phones have capabilities of viewing the person calling in real time; there is satellite broadcasting to capture stations from across the world from the tip of our fingers. Yet couldn't we say that just a century ago these factual events would have been inconceivable?

Our understanding is too incomplete to come to grips with someone as almighty as God. We must think deeply with humbleness before Him because we are the created ones, and He is the Almighty Creator. In Him, all is possible, and Jesus Christ, who came to this world as both man and God through virgin birth, is certainly possible. The prophet Isaiah prophesied Jesus' birth in 700 B.C. as follows: "The virgin will be with a child and will give birth to a son, and (who will be) call[ed] Immanuel" (Isa. 7:14). Even the location of the birth and His role are described in Micah 5:2.

His birth sage was clear, "Repent, for the kingdom of heaven is near." He claimed to be the only way to heaven when He said, "I am the way and the truth and the life and no one comes to the Father except through me" (John 14:6–7). Jesus Christ, who had been much awaited for as prophesied in 749–697 B.C., came into our human history to restore and save all who were born of spiritually contaminated nature.

Because Adam and Eve did not comply within God's system, all generations thereafter bore the effects of their actions—we are all born with inclinations to sin. Because of God's great love for humans, He once again, gave people the opportunity to prosper like Adam and Eve and receive great blessings. This was done through the entry of Christ into the world. God once again defined His expectation, which is to "believe in Him and (in return) receive eternal life" (John 3:16). However, the majority during Christ's time did not accept Jesus as their Savior. Accordingly, the consequence of rejection of Christ brought about horrible tragedy to those who did not believe. While unbelieving Israel as a whole fell under judgment for not complying with God's law, their is a remnant that will be saved (Isa. 6:13; Mal. 4:1–2; Hosea 1:10; Rom. 11:25–27). In the New Testament era, God opened the door of salvation for the Gentiles (everyone except for Israelites) through the apostle Paul's preaching.

Jesus Christ was ultimately crucified for claiming that He was the Son of God. He was crucified as a substitution for us. We deserved God's punishment and wrath because of our sin, but Christ bore God's wrath for us. After His brutal death on the cross, He rose from the dead, thereby conquering death itself. Christ is the true Son of God, the Savior, as the true new light for all of us. In this point, Christ is real and active in working out God's purpose on earth. In Him we can find what the true freedom is, and learn to escape from our miserable ways. In addition we can recover our loss of sense of longing for our eternity.

> The Bible clearly speaks that "Christ is the true light that gives us light to every man was coming into the world."
>
> —John 1:9

CHAPTER ELEVEN

THE PURPOSE OF THE CHURCH AS THE NEW SPIRITUAL COMMUNITY

After Christ's ascension and the majority of Israel was dispersed across the world, the remnant, as a surviving root of Christ, gathered and received the Holy Spirit of God and followed Christ's command to evangelize the world. The message of the cross and Christ's resurrection advanced through the world by the disciples in a mighty fashion. God established a church of both Israelites and Gentiles from all nations whose purpose was and is to witness to people all over the world.

God is going to fulfill His redemptive plans temporarily through the church in Christ as a spiritual and earthly Garden of Eden for believers. Wayne Gruden defines the church as "the community of all true believers for all time, and the picture of the church as God's temple should increase our awareness of God's very presence dwelling in our midst as we meet and begin to experience the blessing of God's rule in their lives."[1] By God's initiative through the gospel, the church is a holy meeting and a spiritual training camp.

The church has been slowly and steadily advancing the kingdom of God throughout the ages as evidenced by the number

---

[1] Wayne Gruden, *Systematic Theology*, pp. 853–859, 864.

of Christian believers throughout the world. God chose His church to be His earthly agent. He has entrusted His church with the gospel and He has promised that not even the gates of hell shall succeed in stopping it.

CHAPTER TWELVE

CHALLENGES

There are various theories on the origin of all things. Those who believe in creation believe the eternal God created the universe and life. In order to deal with the creation of all things—living and non-living—the biblical data gives us a lot of evidence of a Creator and His creative acts. The Bible starts with the declaration statement, "In the beginning God created the heavens and the earth."[1] As such, for creationists, it follows that all the present realities around us are the evidential results of the Creator as the ultimate source of everything.

We claim that the created world consists of complex systems with interrelatedness and interdependence toward a certain goal and that all creatures reproduce only after their own kind, as stated in the Bible. We expect to get watermelons when we plant watermelon seeds. When Adam and Eve conceived, they would have expected to bear a child, not a monkey. Monkeys come from monkeys.

Those who hold to the theory of evolution believe that both organic and inorganic things appear in order of increasing complexity. So the creation and the materialistic evolutionary

[1] Genesis 1:1, NIV.

positions are totally different from their starting points. The creation view has an inspired written record—the Bible—that has historically influenced people's lives. It can be totally trusted. Through careful archaeological and geological evaluations, the Bible has stood the test of time. On the contrary, the atheistic notion of origin has been embraced by far too many people, given that it doesn't have the slightest bit of empirical evidence.

The Evolutionary View

According to the theoretic assumption of the atheistic evolutionary view, the beginning of life was an accidental event that arose from a self-existent non-living material. Through natural selection, uniquely combined chemicals evolved over massive amounts of time into more and more complex organisms, selecting variants among species from lower to higher forms of life. Presumably, mutations occurred and they evolved into modern day man.

The History of Evolution

The philosophers in ancient Greek days contributed a great amount of materialistic mindset to every field of human knowledge in the western hemisphere. Accordingly, Greek thinkers have been responsible for the western mindset for principal reasons in rational and logical ways. They used a methodological technique of questions and answers when considering the origins of the universe, our human values, and our human identity, to explain the natural phenomena on scientific grounds, arriving at fundamental notions about such principles as the atomic composition of matter and its classification into elements.

Thales (640–550 B.C.) identified water as the fundamental source of all things. Leucippus (440 B.C.) and Democritus (429 B.C.) determined that the atom is the basic substance for the composition of the universe and all things. Democritus believed that our soul is composed of atoms; that thought itself was a physical process; and the universe had no supernatural intervention.[2] Lucretius Carus (96–55 B.C.) of Rome recognized there is no place for a supernatural dimension with an intervening deity and that everything obeyed the inexorable laws of chance and nature.[3]

The rationale behind Darwin's theory of evolution is intimately related to the prevailing historical belief system at the time of its conception. The prevailing views among Greek thinkers, later adopted by the Romans, and then in the Middle Ages, inevitably led to the development of different views on the creation of the universe and life. The earth-centered orthodox view of the Latin Church, adopted by Ptolemy of Alexandria (A.D. 85–165)—who was a follower of Aristotle's geocentric theology—was challenged by the Copernican system. It was heliocentric, and asserted by the Polish Latin scholar Nicolas Corpernicus (A.D. 1479–1543). It became evident through Galilleo (A.D. 1564–1642) that geocentricity was in error. That led to warfare between science and theology in the Latin Church.

This period was noted by a humanistic revival expressed in art and literature. By the beginning of modern science, a number of intellectually disciplined thinkers came on the scene such as: Francis Bacon (1561–1626); Rene Descartes (1596–1650); and Francis Marie Arouet Voltaire and Jean Jacques Rousseau (1712–1778). They challenged the teaching of the Latin Church on the doctrine of creation. The discovery of the laws of the universe made a big impact on the beginning of modern science, socialism, and secular humanism. During the eighteenth and nineteenth centuries, the French Revolution

---

[2] Morton Donner, Kenneth E. Eble and Robert E. Helbing, *The Intercultural Tradition of the West*, vol., 1 (Gelnview: Scott, Foresman and Company, 1967). p. 50.

[3] Ian Y. Taylor, *In the Minds of Men,* (Toronto: TEE Publishing, 1987), p. 11.

and the Industrial Revolution of England brought tremendous changes into every field. Key individuals sought to bring the world of nature within the compass of human understanding. Their influence continues on to this very day.

The key people who laid the basis for atheistic and materialistic modern evolution are Comte de Buffon (1707–1788) who proposed, on a broad scale, the mutability of species in relation to changes in environment, and laid the groundwork for atheistic and materialistic evolution in systematic botany and zoology. Buffon sowed the seeds of the idea of atheistic evolution, and these later grew in the minds of his successors. James Hutton (1726–97), who advanced the idea of an evolutionary earth formation, set the stage for Charles Lyell's study and the views of Jean-Baptiste Larmark (1744–1829).

Next came Charles Darwin (1803–82), who proposed a theory of evolution based on natural selection in his treatise, *On the Origin of Species*. He explained the mysteries of the origin of all things from the natural perspective. Darwin's theory said that life began as a simple organism and evolved into more complex organisms, which implies an intelligent directing force, but he wanted to avoid at all cost any kind of inference to the supernatural.[4] This theory of origin was satisfying to people looking for an escape from religious dogma. During this time, Christianity was also declining in scholarly circles as people began to place more confidence in science. The evolutionary idea gradually replaced creation in the field of academics.

---

[4] Ibid., p. 159.

CHAPTER THIRTEEN

DIFFERING WORLDVIEWS

Henry Morris speaks of the harmful influences of the evolutionary idea. He says that "the whole area of the behavior sciences today is thoroughly dominated by evolutionary humanism, and this has resulted in incalculable harm."[1] Under this system, no one can be accused of wrongdoing for behavioral reasons. This idea is dangerous enough to destroy the basic moral fabric of our society.

Experiments with monkeys or other animals (even with insects) are used for guidance in dealing with human problems.[2] If we are only animals, then society must tolerate people acting like animals. Evolution cannot bring eternal hope or ultimate value. Its application brings about more and more harmful influences on our society.

Evolutionists often point to the fossil records as evidence for their cause. But if their theory was correct, we should have an orderly, accurate progression with layer-by-layer fossils. However, evidence does not connect the ladder of living

---

[1] Henry Morris, *The Long War Against God* (Green Forest: Master Books, 2003). pp. 32–36.

[2] Ibid., p. 32.

43

organisms with clear intermediate forms, including people. To this day, no scientist has been able to reproduce the tremendous change between animal and human life.

Granted, there are similarities between different kinds of creatures. We even find that there is a remarkable likeness in the internal body systems, the embryos, and the skeletons of some creatures in relation to people. Because of their likeness, it would seem to justify the evolutionists' position that humans evolved. On the contrary though, we have to consider their similarities are not based on evolution, but instead are designed by a Creator, manifesting a consistent characteristic.

For example, someone may resemble a portrait of his friend's father, but that does not make him his descendant. Instead, we can be sure the similarity conclusively demonstrates that a Creator designed both people with a consistent range of plans. Leonard Sweet, a professor, said:

> We are a part of nature. Just look at our DNA. All of nature is a part of us in that genetic endowment. The fruit fly (Drosophilia melanogaster) shares about 50% of its DNA with humans. In other words flies are 50% of the way to begin human being. Chimpanzees share about 97% of their DNA with humans. The human body is one of the natural wonders of the world . . . What a difference that 3% makes.[3]

God is the almighty Creator, and as such can easily make such distinctions in His creation. Denying His ability to do such creative work is unacceptable. But that's exactly what man has been attempting to do throughout the ages.

If we believe that we are purposeful beings created by God, then we should have a different view of life than those who

---

[3] Leonard Sweed, *Carpe Manana* (Grand Rapids: Zondervan, 2001), p. 160.

believe we are accidents. According to one of the evolutionary ingredients, only the fittest and strongest survive. This idea brings about dangerous results to our world. It means that the physically or mentally challenged person doesn't have any value. The elderly or the sick serve no purpose other than to be preyed upon by those who are young and healthy. The Christian worldview rejects such ridiculous notions and it should bring a moment of clarity to all who consider such situations.

If that isn't enough, then consider these questions:

1. Where did the first matter come from?
2. Where and how did the first life come into being?
3. How do we know that people are an ultimate by-product?
4. Where did the human conscience come from and how did it evolve?
5. Where does one species end and another begin?
6. How has human intelligence developed?
7. Which species evolved into the ape?
8. Where did the first man and woman come from?
9. How could they have evolved into both male and female?
10. Why does it take two—female and male—to create a single offspring?
11. Is the universe an accidental chance?
12. Where did space and time come from?
13. Why does the earth have only enough oxygen for life to survive?
14. Where did gravity come from?
15. Why do the forces of gravity and electricity have the powers that they do? Did they evolve? If so, how?
16. Why is earth the only planet that is fit to inhabit?
17. Why do people live on earth?
18. Why do the different constants of nature have the values that they have?

19. How have all the constants of nature evolved?
20. Why and how does the earth revolve around the sun?
21. Why is the sun earth's only system of heat and light?
22. Why do people look for God?
23. Why do animals have a pair of eyes and ears, and one nose, and one mouth?
24. Why does the tall fruit-tree produce small fruit while the small fruit-tree produces big fruit?
25. Why does mackerel not taste salty even though it lives in the sea?

Additionally, the evolutionary idea cannot easily explain why the nine planets in the solar system, including the earth, need "constant rotation" in reference to their revolution around the sun and why Venus rotates slowly backward. Furthermore, evolutionists have to supply the "how and why" answers to the explanations given by Geoffrey Simmons, a medical doctor, about vision: "Eyelids blink to protect our eyes. Eyeballs roll up at night to protect them from injury when not being used. Tears bring oxygen to the cornea, carry chemicals that kill bacteria and proteins to coat the eyes, wash the eyes, and move debris toward a lower drain, or lacrimal duct."[4] As such, the idea of atheistic and materialistic evolution about the origin of the universe and life raises only new questions that cannot be answered.

In order for an accidental chance to be the origin of life, reproductive living ingredients must be collectively gathered and properly meet in the same location at the same time with tremendous accuracy. Can we imagine these most highly accurate conditions and orderly arrangements are possible from accidental chance? These arrangements or conditions could not bring about the scientifically perfect system of conditions that

---

[4] Simmons, *What Darwin Didn't Know*, p. 55.

are precisely interrelated and interdependent toward a goal. If so, how and where did the first condition come from?

Additionally, "an accidental chance" means that it is only a chance, much like a lottery ticket. It isn't systematically correct or planned or purposeful. Regarding the system of DNA, Stephen C. Meyer, a philosopher, says, "Our experience with information-intensive systems (especially codes and languages) indicates that such systems always come from an intelligent source—i.e., from mental or personal agents, not chance or material necessity."[5] And Jonathan Wells, a biologist, says in his essay that "DNA mutations never alter the endpoint of embryonic development; they cannot even change the species, and the evidence for natural selection has been discredited, and the relevance of industrial melanism to evolution is in doubt."[6] Cornelius Hunter, a scientist, says that life cell machinery uses the genetic code to interpret the information stored in the DNA molecule when creating proteins with making use of the same code, not following accidental blind chance.[7]

This means that the function of the life cell is not dependent upon accidental chance, but depends upon a perfect systemic planned regularity. If accidental chance evolves, then presumably the cycle of life would eventually stop. The end point for atheistic evolution, therefore, is one of a meaningless and purposeless human existence. But we know better than that. The theory of accidental chance by mutation or natural selection has been shown to be statistically impossible, and does not make any sense at all.

All evidences confirm that an intelligent Creator, the God of the Bible, designed and created the universe and all living

---

[5] Phillip E. Johnson, Michael Behe, Nancy Pearcy, and Others, *Signs of Intelligence: Understanding intelligent Design* edited by William A. Demski & James M. Kushiner (Grand Rapids: Brazos Press, 2001). p. 115.
[6] Ibid., p. 123.
[7] Cornelius G. Hunter, *Darwin's God* (Grand Rapids Press, 2001), p. 24.

things. The Bible clearly indicates different kinds of creatures. Consider 1 Corinthians 15:38–39: "God gives it a body as He has determined, and to each kind of seed He gives its own body. All flesh is not the same: Men have one kind of flesh, animals have another, birds another and fish another." Therefore, we cannot agree that evolution is scientifically an ultimate and true explanation and that furthermore, it cannot have a clear explanation and criteria on what sin and death are. Evolution cannot explain the origin of the universe and life, and depends upon hypothetical evidences that are utterly hopeless and willfully obstinate toward God and His created works.

CHAPTER FOURTEEN

THE DIVINELY INSPIRED BIBLE

Throughout human history, the Bible is the most spiritually and practically influential guidance book ever written. It has also been read more widely than any other book in history. The Bible was written by thirty-six to forty people from various walks of life, covering a 1,500 year period of time, from Moses (1440 B.C.) to the apostle John (A.D. 90). The Bible consists of thirty-nine books in the Old Testament and twenty-seven books in the New Testament. All of the authors were inspired by the Holy Spirit (2 Pet. 1:21; 2 Tim. 3:16; Heb. 1:1–2) and state their writings were not their own intentional words.

The purposeful Word of God contains His law as spiritual food, and gives us access to the present and future blessing of the kingdom of God (Exod. 34:27; Jer. 25:1–25; 3 John 1:2). The Bible gives us the ultimate answers to questions about our origins and about eternity. It defines morality for us. And the Bible contains narrations from eternity past before creation (John 1:2) to eternity future (Rev. 22:5) with continuity, oneness, and accord.

We must pay attention to the constant repetition of such expressions as: "The Lord said . . .;" "The word of the Lord came unto . . .;" and "Jesus said. . . ." Such phrases are found in every book of the Bible, giving full evidence that the whole Bible is the Word of God. There are also many prophetic expressions that did not come by the will of people, but by the will of God (2 Pet. 1:21). Many scientists have verified the Word of God by investigations and many archaeologists have proved the Word of God by historical discoveries. Incalculable people throughout world history have enjoyed, been impressed by, and have been changed into spiritually new creatures by reading the Word of God.

The main theme of the whole Bible is Christ—the Savior of all sinners, who turn to Him (John 1:12). Only the Bible brings about a purposeful hope, a vision of opportunity, room for engaging in multi-cultural groups, healthy families, the spirit of discipline and patience, the true and successful value of work and life, and a firm foundation of eternal faith for our present and future—all through the merits of Jesus Christ (John 14:2–4).

Thomas Carlyle deeply expressed: "There never was a Book like the Bible and there never will be any other such book."[1] Voltaire, the infidel, said: "Twelve men started Christianity, but one man will destroy it and I will be that one man. Within one hundred years, only a few old Bibles will be found in the museum." Those hundred years have passed, and he was wrong. At an auction sale, the whole of Voltaire's works (91 volumes) were sold for $1.41, while the British Government purchased a portion of the Bible—the Codex Siniaticus—for $700,000, the greatest price ever paid for a book.[2]

---

[1] C. W. Slemming, *The Bible Digest* (Grand Rapids: Kregel Publications, 1960), p. 16.
[2] Ibid., p. 16.

The Reliability of the Bible

Truth is based on historical facts. Reliability is based on truth. Therefore, truth brings about reliability. Many people, even some Christians, have questioned of the reliability of the Bible based on historical fact as the Word of God. But there are plenty of evidences to support its reliability. In order to find convincing historical evidence, we depend upon several things: the testimony of eyewitnesses and opposed groups at the time; archaeological digs; the analysis of prophetical fulfillments; and finally, the Bible itself.

Eyewitnesses

Eyewitness and writers during biblical times came from various backgrounds, locations, and time periods (from about 1440 B.C. to A.D. 90). But their writing themes were consistent throughout the Bible. How could that be, given their varying circumstances, locations and different ages? They did not have any burning awareness of the existence of God until they saw Christ's resurrection and were spiritually moved and inspired.

We see common themes, such as: God being heralded as the Creator; the fall of man and its effects; the coming Messiah who would save people from their sins; the birth, life, death, resurrection, and ascension of the Messiah; His simple, yet costly, plan of salvation; the second coming of Christ; and the final judgment.

Here are some of the eyewitnesses who spoke about such themes: Moses (1440 B.C.), Joshua (1400 B.C.), Samuel (1000 B.C.), David (1000 B.C.), Solomon (970 B.C.), Amos (860 B.C.), Isaiah (740–700 B.C.), Micah (749–697 B.C.), Jeremiah (626–586 B.C.), Daniel (606–534 B.C.), Mark (A.D. 62–68), Matthew (A.D. 68), Luke (A.D. 60), John (A.D. 80–90), Peter (A.D. 63), James (A.D. 62), and Paul, the former enemy of Christianity (A.D. 45–65). There are also countless other eyewitnesses.

As a by-product of what they saw, many Old Testament and New Testament saints were willing to suffer martyrdom. Their beliefs were based on historical facts and their experiences, not just from their own ideas. Many saw the ministerial life, historical torture, and crucifixion of Jesus Christ with their own eyes. They themselves were the primary source of all the factual situations. Would martyrs be willing to die for something they believed to be untrue?

The non-Christian eyewitnesses include: Josephus, a first century Jewish historian (A.D. 64–93); Cornelius Tacitus (A.D. 64–116), an early second century Roman historian; Lucian of Samosata, a mid-second century Greek historian; Mara Bar Seyapion, a second to third century prisoner who wrote letters to his son; and Thallus. Additionally, in the first century, Seneca described a man hanging on a cross as being "sickly," and swollen with "ugly welts on the shoulders and chest."[3]

All of these people lived during the time in which Jesus was crucified and many of them had reasons to muddy the waters. As unbelievers, why would they want to validate that Jesus was who He said He was? They probably didn't, but their desire to record their experiences accurately outweighed their own personal biases. Therefore, we can accept that their testimonies about Jesus' crucifixion were accurate.

The fact that so many of these people were eyewitnesses of the resurrection and ascension of Jesus means a lot. The resurrection is the crux of the Christian faith. Paul recognized this when he said, "If Christ has not been raised, our preaching is useless and so is your faith" (1 Cor. 15:14).

The Bible has its own strong credibility. Reliable sources for the credibility of the Bible came from the gospels of Matthew, Mark, and John. And the book of Acts gives us background

---

[3] Quoted from Michael R. Licona, *The Evidence for Jesus' Resurrection in the Big Argument: Does God Exist?* by John Ashton and Michael Westacott (Green Forest: Master Books, 2006), p. 362.

evidence. Jesus had his doubters. Remember Doubting Thomas? He said, "Unless I can put my finger into the nail wounds in His hands and my hand into His side, I will not believe" (John 20:23–29). Thomas carefully examined the evidence of His hands and side. Then he fell down in worship: "My Lord and my God" (John 20:28).

The apostle Paul's story adds even more credibility to the Bible. In the book of Acts, Luke portrays Paul as an aggressive persecutor of the Christian church, but after an encounter with God on the road to Damascus (Acts 8–9), he turned to the faith, and began to preach about the validity of the risen Christ. Paul was eventually martyred for his faith by Nero, the Emperor of Rome, in A.D. 66. He was one of the most historically reliable people and personally knew the disciples of Jesus Christ.

The apostle Peter bore witness to the fact that Jesus rose from the dead (Acts 2:32). James, the half brother of Jesus, who did not initially believe that Jesus was the Christ, became convinced and ended up as a strong faithful leader in the Jerusalem church by seeing Christ's resurrection (Acts 15:12–21; Gal. 1:19; 1 Cor. 9:5). Paul called James "the Lord's brother" (Gal. 1:19), and James wrote that he himself was "a servant of God and of the Lord Jesus Christ" (James 1:1). Stephen was stoned for believing that Jesus was who He said He was (Acts 6; 7:59–60). Again I ask: Who would die for an idea they believed to be false?

Clement of Rome wrote a letter to the Corinthian church around A.D. 95–96. He reported that the disciples had been "fully assured by the resurrection of our Lord, Jesus Christ" and as a result preached the good news of God's kingdom. Many of the early church fathers spoke about the resurrection and deity of Christ: Polycarp (A.D. 69–155), who was believed to be a disciple of John; Justin Martyr ("He is even . . . God." A.D. 160); Ignatius ("God Himself was manifested in human form." A.D. 105); Tertullian ("Christ our God." A.D. 150–222);

and Origen ("No one should be offended that the Savior is also God." A.D. 185–253).

Non-Christian Testimonies

Josephus, as a leading Jewish historian (A.D. 64–94) said:

> Now there was about this time, Jesus, a wise man, if it be lawful to call him a man, for he was a doer of wonderful works . . . He was Christ; and when Pilate, at the suggestion of the principal men amongst us, had condemned Him to the cross, those that loved Him at the first did not forsake Him, for He appeared to them alive again the third day, as divine prophets had foretold these.[4]

From the record of Cornelius Tacitus (A.D. 64–116), Josh McDowell provides early non-Christian references to Jesus as follows:

> He was falsely charged with the guilt, and punished with the most exquisite tortures, Christus, the founder of the name, was put to death by Pontius Pilate, procurator of Judea in the reign of Tiberius: But the pernicious superstition, repressed for a time, broke out again, not only through Judea, where the mischief originated, but through the city of Rome also.[5]

> Thallus, in a historical work that was referenced by Julius Africanus, had mistakenly claimed there was a solar eclipse at the time of Jesus' death, trying to

---

[4] Flavius Josephus, *The Complete Works of Josephus* (Grand Rapids: Kregel Publications, 1999), p. 988.

[5] As cited by Josh McDowell, *A Ready* Defence compiled by Bill Wilson (San Bernardino, CA: Here's Publishers, 1990), p. 198.

explain the darkness that fell during the crucifixion. Africanus points out in a letter that no such
eclipse occurred. The death of Jesus was stated as
a matter of fact. In this statement we can find that
there was a miraculous event at the place of Christ's
crucifixion.[6]

Archaeological Evidence

As you probably know, archaeology is the study of the material remains of our past. The material remains of the ancient
palaces, temples, inscribed stones, coins, and copies of writings
that have been excavated by archaeologists allow us to understand the historical, social, cultural, political, economic, and
religious backgrounds of the past.

Professor Paul E. Little states that more than 25,000 ancient
sites showing some connection with the Old Testament period
have been located in the Bible lands.[7] Archaeology is an important tool we can use to confirm and verify the reliability of written records, including the Bible. There are plenty of evidences
to confirm the credibility of biblical records by archaeological
discoveries. Here are some selected examples.

The Old Testament

The ancient city of Babylon was rebuilt in Iraq. From September
22–October 22, 1987, the Babylon International Festival featuring king Nebuchadnezzar was held at the reconstructed site. And
the ancient cities of Jerusalem in Israel and Damascus in Syria
described in Genesis 14:15 and Acts 9 currently remain today.

---

[6] Ralph O. Muncaster, *A Skeptic's Search for God* (Eugene: Harvest House
Publishers, 2002), p. 218.

[7] Quoted from Paul E. Little, *Know Why You Believe* (Downers Grove:
InterVarsity, 2000), p. 87.

Genesis 11:31 refers to Abraham's home town called "Ur." It was discovered by C.L. Wooly in 1936.[8] According to information at the archaeological survey, the biblical setting of Abraham's time period is very similar to those known from the cities of Mari and Nuzi. The discovery of those cities gives us new information about the ancient Mesopotamian cultures and gives us an additional picture of the urban lifestyles of Abraham's time period in relation to the biblical records. The discoveries of these cities reflect social customs and relationships that parallel the situations found in the patriarchal society in the Old Testament.

There have been thousands of tablets discovered by archaeologists at Mari close to the Euphrates River that gave us much information on ancient civilizations with evidences of similarities to nomadic culture from the time of Hebrew patriarchs in the Bible. Mark W. Chavalas, a history professor, and K. Lawson Younger, Jr., an Old Testament professor, explain that, "One area of study that has been explored fairly in recent years is the possible comparisons that could be made between the ancestral narratives of Genesis and the Mari texts that describe the interaction between the government and pastoral nomadic tribal groups."[9] The excavated remains and properties give us an idea about patriarchal life, the political movements, the cultural and business activities of these cities, and more.

More excavated tablets at Nuzi, located east of the city of Mari, show private adoption contracts similar to the situation of Abraham's adoption of Eliezer and the barrenness and remarriage for an heir which are found in Genesis 15–16. According to tablets, the natural son always had the first priority in any situations. A similar case is written in Genesis 16:1–2. Sarah, as Abraham's wife, who had not borne him children, recommends that her

---

[8] Mark W. Chavalas and K. Lawson Younger, Jr., *Mesopotamia and the Bible*, (Grand Rapids: Baker Academic, 2002), p. 35.
[9] Ibid., p.172.

husband have a child through her maidservant, Hagar. Alfred Hoerth and John MacRay, professors of archaeology, mention a tablet dealing with the right of a married man who has no children, "The man was free to divorce his wife and remarry, but the childless couple also had the option to adopt."[10]

The particular tablet of Nuzi and the Hamurabi Law Code require that the slave's child be kept—a rule which was preempted by the divine command to send Hagar and Ishmael away according to Edwin M. Yamauch, a professor of archaeology.[11]

An inscribed stone found by a German named Klein in 1868 at Dibon of the land of Moab shows that Omri, the king of Israel, is referred to by name in the inscription along with a number of biblical places. Significantly, it mentions the God of Israel, as "Yahweh."[12]

We also have the Old Testament city of Hazor and its king, Jabin, mentioned in Joshua 11:1,10. Hazor is about ten miles north of the Sea of Galilee. It was one of the largest cities in Israel. It occupied approximately two hundred acres and may have had a population of about thirty thousand people.[13] Hazor and its king's name are described in excavated Mari tablets, and the city is referred to as a center for caravans in the metal trade. Its king's name is described as Ibni-Addu. Abraham Malamat mentions that in the west this would have been pronounced Yabni-Addu, translated from an older Hebrew word "Yabnu."[14]

Walter C. Kaiser Jr., an Old Testament scholar, points out this about Abraham's relatives:

---

[10] Alfred Hoerth and John MacRay, *Bible Archaeology* (Grand Rapids: Baker Books, 2005), p. 106.
[11] Paul E. Little, *Know Why You Believe*, p. 91.
[12] Ibid., p. 95.
[13] Quoted from Paul Ferguson, *The Historical Reliability of the Old Testament in the Big Argument,* p. 274.
[14] Ibid., p. 275.

His great-grand father was named Serug, his father Nahor, and his father Terah. Studies that have come from Old Assyrian, Babylonian and Neo-Assyrian texts confirm the fact that these names appear in documents that report events belonging to this same era and coming from the Euphrates-Habur region of Upper Mesopotamia. Since the biblical accounts link Abraham and his line with this very area around Haran where he temporarily settled after moving from Ur of the Chaldees, the connection is more than a mere accident.[15]

We have the records of Jonah's mission to Nineveh. Jonah, the Hebrew prophet, was divinely commissioned to go to Nineveh. He thought it was a dangerous and complicated mission so he refused the order and took a trip in the opposite direction. As the book of Jonah describes, God brought him back, "For this proclamation of Jonah, there comes with the king's repentance of Nineveh; 'He rose from his throne, took off his royal robes, covered himself with sackcloth and sat down in the dust'" (Jon. 3:5–6).

Many liberals have questioned this event. How did a great Assyrian king get up from his throne, removing his royal robes, and sit in the dust? But reports that have been published by the University of Helsinki confirm it to be true. The following quotation is taken from a letter titled *the king must give up fasting*: "The king, our lord, will pardon us. Is one day not enough for the king to mope and to eat nothing? . . . This is the third day (when) the king does not eat anything. The king is beggar."[16]

---

[15] Walter C. Kaiser Jr., *The Old Testament Documents* (Downers Grove: InterVarsity Press, 2001), p. 88.
[16] Quoted from Paul Ferguson, *The Historical Reliability of the Old Testament in the Big Argument*, pp. 284–286.

Then we have the interesting records of the ten plagues in Egypt for Israel's emancipation in Exodus 7–11. Some question whether those plagues actually occurred. Was the water of the Nile River really changed into blood and the first born of every Egyptian killed? David K. Down points to "a papyrus written in a later period well kept in the Leiden Museum in Holland but which most scholars recognize as being a copy of a papyrus from an earlier dynasty."[17]

The New Testament

The reliability of the New Testament depends primarily upon written documents as evidence, unlike the Old Testament. It is reasoned that the period covered by New Testament history is too long for archaeology to be as helpful as it has been with the Old Testament history, which covers a period of about 1,500 years. However, archaeology is still very supportive. For up to twenty years after the ascension of Jesus Christ, there were no New Testament books.

The first New Testament eyewitness authors were Matthew, Mark, John, Peter, and James. Then came Paul and his companion, Luke. While their original manuscripts were passed from church to church, they were also copied, and then either the original or the copies or both would be circulated. Thus, the Gospels and the Epistles could be obtained by individuals and by churches.

However, before anyone could obtain a Bible like the one we have today, it had to be carefully screened by the early church and church councils for possible mistakes that scribes could have made while making copies. Eventually the Bible was canonized, and ever since then it has been relied upon as the inerrant Word of God.

---

[17] Quoted from David K. Dowcon, *Archaeological Evidence for the Exodus in the Big Argument*, p. 268.

We also have supportive archaeological excavations. A number of geological sites mentioned in the New Testament give us even more confidence in the accuracy and reliability of the New Testament. When I visited Israel, I found that my faith in the Bible was strengthened even more.

Here are a few excavated sites from the New Testament:

1. Jerusalem has lots of caves, the city walls, and the closed east-gate wall.
2. The Jericho wall (Mark 10:46).
3. The Sea of Galilee and the Jordan River.
4. The pool of Siloam (John 9:7) in southern Jerusalem.
5. The Capernaum Synagogue (Matt. 4:13; Mark 1:21, 2:1, 3:1; Luke 4:23).
6. The city of Bethlehem, the birthplace of Jesus Christ.
7. The remains of the Peter's house.
8. The site of Caesarea.
9. The tomb of Lazarus in Bethany.
10. Gethsemane, the place where Jesus prayed.
11. The tomb of Caiaphas.
12. The site of the ruins of Laodicea as the last of the seven cities.
13. The tomb of Herod.

Fulfilled Prophecies

One of the strongest evidences for the reliability of the Bible is the phenomenon of fulfilled prophecy. The Bible is unique among the religious documentations of peoples in that it vividly predicts future events in detail.

While the Old Testament can be considered a shadow of the future plans of God, the New Testament is a decisive portion of the realized plans of God through the world in Christ. According to statistics:

Out of the Old Testament's 23,210 verses, 6,641 verses are predictive ones with 28.5 percent, and 1,711 verses out of the total 7,914 verses of the New Testament are predictive ones with 21.5 percent. For the both Testaments 31,124 verses, 8,352 verses are predictive with 27 percent of the both testaments (the whole Bible).[18]

All of this prophecy proves that God is involved in human history.

Some prophecies were applied to individuals, some to certain locations, some to churches, and some to nations. Some prophecies referred to immediate situations, and some referred to events far in the future. Therefore, in order to search for the credibility and reliability of the Bible, we have to carefully examine whether the prophecies of the Bible are to be realized or not. Why base our eternal resting place upon a book that is not trustworthy?

According to Genesis 3, God sets the plan of salvation in motion after Adam and Eve fall into sin. The Messiah would come through Abraham's seed. Later in the Bible we read the writing of Isaiah who says that the Messiah will be born of a virgin (Isa. 7:7–14). Of course, Isaiah was correct.

Here are several more selected biblical prophecies and their realizations as they are related to Christ:

> *Prediction*: "The woman's seed shall bruise the serpents head, and serpent should bruise his heel" (Gen. 3:15). In this verse, the woman's seed symbolizes Christ, and the serpent's head Satan. "Heel" refers to Christ's sufferings on the cross.

---

[18] J. Barton Payn, *Encyclopedia of Biblical Prophecy*, (Grand Rapids: Baker Book House, 1973), p. 681.

Realization: Serpent's bruising His heel is a symbolical reference to the Christ's sufferings and death with being wounded for humans' sins, and the seed of the woman shall bruise the serpent's head is Christ's resurrection out of the dead and Christ's second coming in person and in power, and cast the evil force into the bottomless pit.

—Revelation 20:2–3

Prediction: "I offered my back to those who beat me, my cheeks to those pulled out my beard; I did not hide my face from mocking and spitting."

—Isaiah 50:6

Realization: "Then they spit in His face and struck Him with their fists. Others slapped Him."

—Matthew 26:67

Prediction: "He was oppressed and afflicted, yet He did not open His mouth; He was led like a lamb to the slaughter, and as a sheep before her shearers is silent, so he did not open His mouth."

—Isaiah 53:7

Realization: "When He was accused by the chief priest and the elders, He gave no answer. Pilate who was a proconsul of Roman Empire asked Him, 'Don't you hear the testimony they are bringing against you?' But Jesus made no reply, not even to a single charge to the great amazement of the governor."

—Matthew 27:12–14

Prediction: "He will receive the obedience of the peoples."

—Genesis 49:10

Realization: "The crowds that went ahead of Him and those that followed shouted, 'Hosanna to the son of David! Blessed is He who comes in the name of the Lord! Hosanna in the highest'" (Matt. 21:9), and today, too.

Prediction: "O, daughter of Jerusalem: behold, your king come to you, righteous and having salvation, gentile and riding on a donkey, on a colt, the foal of a donkey."

—Zechariah 9:9

Realization: "They brought it to Jesus, threw their cloaks on the colt and put Jesus on it. As He went along, people spread their cloaks on the road. When He came near the place where the road goes down the Mount of Olives, the whole crowd of disciples began joyfully to praise God in loud voices for all the miracles they had seen."

—Luke 19:35–37

Prediction: "If you think it best, give me my pay; but if not, keep it." So they paid thirty pieces of silver" (Zech. 11:12).

Realization: And asked, "What are you willing to give me if I hand over to you?" So they counted out for him thirty coins.

—Matthew 26:15

Prediction: And the Lord said to me, "Throw it to the potter"—the handsome price at which they priced me! So I took the thirty pieces of silver and threw them into the house of the Lord to the potter.

—Zechariah 11:13

Realization: "So Jude threw the money into the temple and left. Then he went away and hanged himself. The chief priests picked up the coins and said, 'It is blood money.' So they decided to use the money to buy the potter's field as a burial place for foreigners."

—Matthew 27:1–8

Prediction: "Even my close friend, whom I trusted, he who shared my bread, had lifted up his heel against me."

—Psalm 41:9

Realization: Now the betrayer had arranged a signal with them: "The one I kiss is the man; arrest Him. Going at once to Jesus, Judah said, 'Greetings Rabbi!' and kissed Him."

—Matthew 26:48–49

Prediction: "The kings of the earth take their stand and the rulers gather against the Lord and against his anointed one."

—Psalm 2:2

Realization: "All the chief priests and the elders of the people came to decision to put Jesus to death."

—Matthew 27:1

Prediction: "But He was pierced for our transgression, He was crushed for our iniquities; the punishment that brought us peace was upon Him; and by His wounds we are healed."

—Isaiah 53:5

Realization: "Then he released Barabas to them. But he had Jesus flogged, and handed Him over to be crucified."

—Matthew 27:26

Prediction: "Dogs have surrounded me; a band of evil men have encircled me, they have pierced my hands and my feet."

—Psalm 22:16

Realization: "When they came to the place called the skull (Calvary), they crucified Him, along with the criminals."

—Luke 23:33; John 19:18

Prediction: "Because he poured out his life unto death, and was numbered with the transgressors. For He bore the sin of many, and made intercession for the transgressors."

—Isaiah 53:12

Realization: "Two robbers were crucified with Jesus, one on His right and one on His left."

—Matthew 27:38; Luke 23:33

Prediction: "They put gall in my food and gave me vinegar for my thirst."

—Psalm 69:21

Realization: "There they offered Jesus wine to drink, mixed with gall; but after tasting it, He refused to drink it."

—Matthew 27:34

Prediction: "He protects all his bones, not one of them will be broken."

—Psalm 34:20

Realization: "These things happened so that the scripture would be fulfilled: Not one of His bones will be broken."

—John 19:36

Prediction: "And he made his grace with the wicked, and with the rich in His death."

—Isaiah 53:9

Realization: "There came a rich man of Arimathaea, named Joseph, who also himself was Jesus' disciple: He went to Pilate, and begged the body of Jesus. Then Pilate commanded the body to be delivered . . . And laid it in his own new tomb, which he had hewn out in the rock; and rolled a great stone to the door of the sepulcher, and departed."

—Matthew 27:57–60

Prediction: "But the angel said to her, do not be afraid, Mary, you have found favor with God. You will be with child and give birth to a son, and you are to give him the name Jesus."

—Luke 1:30–31

Realization: "And she gave birth to her first born, a son. She wrapped him in cloths and placed him in a manger, because there was no room for them in the inn."

—Luke 2:7; Matthew 2:10–11

Prediction: "From that time on Jesus began to explain to His disciples that He must go to Jerusalem and suffer many things at the hands of the elders, chief priests and teachers of the law, and that He must be killed and on the third day be raised to life."

—Matthew 16:21

Realization: "He is not here; he has risen, just as He said. Come and see the place where He lay."

—Matthew 28:7; Mark 16:6;
Luke 24:6; John 20:6–7; Acts 9:4)

Prediction: "All the people answered, 'Let His blood be on us and on our children.'"

—Matthew 27:25

Realization: The Jews experienced severe hardship worldwide from A.D. 70 till May 14, 1948.

Prediction: "The Lord had said to Abram, 'Leave your country, your people and your father's household and go to the land I will show you. I will make you into a great nation and I will bless you.'"

—Genesis 12:1–2

Realization: "So, I gave you a land on which you did not toil and cities you did not build; and you live in them and eat from vineyards and olive groves that you did not plant."

—Joshua 24:13

Prediction: "If you then become corrupt and make any kind of idol, doing in the eyes of the lord your God. The Lord will scatter you among the peoples, and only a few of you will survive among the nations to which the Lord will drive you . . . You will become a thing of horror and an object of scorn and ridicule to all the nations where the Lord will drive you."

—Deuteronomy 4:27, 28:37; Jeremiah 25:11

Realization: "In the thirtieth year, in the fourth month on the fifth day, while among the exiles by the Kebar River, the heavens were opened and I saw visions of God."

—Ezekiel 1:1; Daniel 1 and from after Christ's ascension to May 14, 1948

Prediction: "Prophesy to these bones and say to them, 'Dry bones, hear the word of the Lord.' This is what the sovereign Lord says to these bones: 'I will make breath enter you, and you will come to life. I will attach tendons to you and make flesh come upon you and cover you with skin.' . . . Then you will know that I am the Lord. So I prophesied as I was commanded. And as I was prophesying, there was a noise, a rattling sound, and the bones came together, bone to bone . . . Then He said to me: 'Son of man, these bones are the whole house of Israel . . . Therefore prophesy and say to them: "O my people, I am going to open your graves and bring you up from them. I will bring you back to the land of Israel."'"

—Ezekiel 37:4–12

Realization: After Christ's ascension, Israel was scattered all over the world until May 14, 1948.

Prediction: "But the subject of the kingdom will be thrown outside, into the darkness, where there will be weeping and gnashing of teeth."

—Matthew 8:12

Realization: After Christ's ascension, Israel was scattered all over the world and under severe persecution by nations through out until May 14, 1948.

CHAPTER FIFTEEN

DISPERSION AND REBIRTH OF ISRAEL

Throughout the Old Testament, Israel continued to fall into sin. Eventually they were taken into captivity by Assyria and Babylonia. God said through the prophet that Israel would be held captive in Babylon for seventy years (Jer. 25:12, 29:10). They were released at the end of the seventy-year period under King Cyrus of the Persian Empire who defeated the Babylonians in 536 B.C. Some of the people of Israel returned to their homeland (2 Chron. 36:22–23) and some were scattered throughout the region. The prophecy of Jeremiah came true.

Despite their spiritual turmoil, they continued to hold out hope for the promised Messiah (Isa. 7:14). God gave Israel many chances to repent. Even after they did, they always fell back into sin. And even after Jesus arrived on the scene, many of them rejected Him. This consequence of rejecting Christ as their Redeemer brought serious consequences. The temple was destroyed and numerous inhabitants in Jerusalem were killed by the Romans under the leadership of Titus. This scattered them even further.

However, even during their tragic dispersions, they met subsequent persecutions everywhere they went. And of course, their leaders eventually put Jesus to death, which took them out of favor with early church leaders. Justin Martyer (A.D. 167) and Origen (A.D. 251) accused Israel of plotting to kill Christians. Eusebius (A.D. 300) asserted that Israel engaged in the ceremonial murder of Christian children at the holiday of Purim. Chrysostom (A.D. 344–407) mentioned that "There could never be expiation for the Jews," and that "God had always hated them," because of their killing of Christ. Jerome (420 A.D.) said that Jews were "incapable of understanding the Scripture, and that they should be severely persecuted until they were forced to confess the true faith."

The 15th and 16th centuries were tragic periods for the scattered Jews. Hundreds of thousands of Israelites were killed by the leaders of inquisitions. In Russia there were tremendous persecutions against Israel under the name of "pogrom," which means destruction. This persecution caused Israel to run into Germany, where six million of them were massacred under the Hitler regime in the twentieth century.

Hitler had women's hair cut off and used in the manufacturing of clothing and mattresses. Bodies were used to make inexpensive soap. The ashes of the cremated were used as fertilizer. The few who survived these horrors have told their stories and they are difficult to listen to. How could these unspeakable things happen?

The answer can be found in Matthew 23:37–38: "O Jerusalem, Jerusalem, you who kill the prophets and stone those sent to you, how often I have longed to gather your children together, as a hen gathers her chicks under her wings, but you were not willing, look your house is left to you desolate." Israel even went so far as to want to put Jesus to death, saying, "Let His blood be on us and on our children!" in Matthew 27:25.

Israel was commissioned to carry God's redemptive plan to the world, but they have continually fallen short. Here are some of the predicted biblical dispersions and hardships:

> If you remain hostile toward me and refuse to listen to me, I'll multiply your afflictions seven times over, as your sins deserve. I will send you wild animals against you, and they will rob you of your children . . . I will scatter you among the nations . . . your land will be laid waste, and your cities will be in ruins . . . As for those of you who are left, I will make their hearts so fearful in the lands of their enemies that the sound of a windblown leaf will put them to fight. You will be perished among the nations; the land of your enemies will devour you. Those of you who are left will waste away in the lands of their enemies because of their sins; also because of their father's sins they will waste away.
>
> —Leviticus 26:21–39

> However, if you do not obey the Lord your God and do not carefully follow all His commands and decrees I am giving you today, all these curses will come upon you and overtake you . . . The Lord will cause to be defeated before your enemies. You will come at them from one direction but flee from them in seven, and you will become a thing of horror to all kingdoms on earth . . . Then the Lord will scatter you among all nations, from one end of the earth to the other. There you will worship other gods—gods of wood and stone, which neither you or your fathers have known.
>
> —Deuteronomy 28:12–25,64

The Lord said, "It is because they have forsaken my law, which I set before them, they have not obeyed me or followed my law. Instead, they have followed the stubbornness of their hearts; they have followed the Baal . . . I will make this people eat bitter food and drink poisoned water. I will scatter them among nations that neither they nor their fathers have known, and I will purpose them with the sword until I have destroyed them."

—Jeremiah 9:13–16

My mountain in the land and your wealth and all your treasures I will give away as plunder, together with your high places, because of sin throughout your country. Through your own fault you will lose the inheritance I gave you. I will enslave you to your enemies in a land you do not know, for you have kindled my anger, and it will burn forever.

—Jeremiah 17:3–4

I will pursue them with the sword, famine and plague and will make them abhorrent to all the kingdoms of the earth and an object of cursing and horror, of scorn and reproach, among all the nations where I drive them.

—Jeremiah 29:18–19

But I will spare some, for some of you will escape the sword when you are scattered among the lands and nations.

—Ezekiel 6:8

I dispersed them among the nations, and they were scattered through the countries; I judged them according to their conduct and their actions.

—Ezekiel 36:19

My God will reject them because they have not obeyed Him; they will be wanderers among the nations.

—Hosea 9:17

Therefore this is what the Lord says: "Your wife will become a prostitute in the city, and your sons and daughters will fall by the sword. Your land will be measured and divided up, and you yourself will die in a pagan country."

—Amos 7:17

But the subject of the kingdom will be thrown outside, into the darkness, where there will be weeping and gnashing of teeth.

—Matthew 8:12

O Jerusalem, Jerusalem, you who kill the prophets and stone those sent to you, how often I have longed to gather your children together, as a hen gathers her chicks under her wing, but you were not willing. Look, your house is left to you desolate.

—Matthew 23:37–38

When you see Jerusalem being surrounded by armies, you will know that its desolation is near . . . They will fall by the sword and will be taken as prisoners to all the nations. Jerusalem will be trampled on until the times of Gentiles are fulfilled, (Luke 21:20–24). Even today part of Jerusalem city belongs to Palestine.

"Do you see all these things?" He asked, "I tell you the truth, not one stone here will be left on another; every one will be thrown down."

—Matthew 24:2

"Why? What crime has He committed?" asked Pilate. But they shouted all the louder, "Crucify Him!" When Pilate saw that he was getting nowhere, but that instead an uproar was starting, he took water and washed his hands in front of the crowd. "I am innocent of this man's blood," he said. "It is your responsibility!" All the people answered, "Let His blood be on us and on our children!"

—Matthew 27:23–25

"Do you refuse to speak to me?" Pilate said. "Don't you realize I have power either to free you or to crucify you?" Jesus answered, "You would have no power over me if it were not given to you from above. Therefore the one who handed me over to you is guilty of a great sin."

—John 19:10–11

Despite Israel's fallen state, God had a plan for them to return to their homeland. On May 14, 1948, Israel initiated their declaration of independence and for the first time in two thousand years they were home again. This event was an unimaginable miracle, and indicates yet again that God has been involved in history. Here are some of the prophecies that spoke about God's bringing Israel back to their homeland:

And when you and your children return to the Lord, your God and obey Him with all your heart and with all your soul according to everything I command thee (you) today, then the Lord your God will restore your captivity and have compassion. And you shall return unto the Lord your God, and shall obey His voice according to all that I command you this day, you and your children, with all your heart, and with all your soul; That then, the Lord your God will turn your captivity, and have compassion upon you, and will return and gather you from all the nations, wither the Lord your God has scattered you . . . And the Lord your God will bring you into the land which your fathers passed, and you shall possesses it; and He will do you good, and multiply the above your fathers.

—Deuteronomy 30:2–5

"So do not fear, O Jacob my servant; do not be dismayed, O Israel," declares the Lord. "I will surely save you out of a distant place, your descendants from the land of their exile."

—Jeremiah 30:10

Therefore say: "This is what the sovereign Lord says; I will gather you from the nations and bring you back from the countries where you have been scattered, and I will give you back the land of Israel again."

—Ezekiel 11:17

As a shepherd looks after his scattered flocks when he is with them, so I will look after my sheep. I will reduce them from the place where they were scattered on a day of clouds and darkness.

—Ezekiel 34:12

For I will take you out of the nations; I will gather you from all the countries and bring you back into your own land.

—Ezekiel 36:24

Therefore, prophesy and say to them: "This is what the Sovereign Lord says: O my people, I am going to open your graves and bring you up from them; I will bring you back to the land of Israel."

—Ezekiel 37:12

I will make one nation in the land, on the mountains of Israel. There will be one king over all of them and they will never be two nations or divided into two kingdoms.

—Ezekiel 37:22

I will bring back my exiled people of Israel; they will rebuild the ruined cities and live in then they will plant vineyards and drink their wines; they will make gardens and eat their fruit. I will plant Israel in their own land, never again to be uprooted from the land I have given them.

—Amos 9:14–15

At that time will I bring you again, even in the time that I gather you: for I will make you a name and a praise among all people of the earth, when I turn back your captivity before your eyes, said the Lord.

—Zephaniah 3:20

So when they met together, they asked Him, 'Lord, are you at this time going to restore the kingdom of Israel?' He (Jesus) said to them (disciples): 'It is not for you to know the times or dates the Father has set by His own authority' (Acts 1:6–7). Almost two thousand years later, this question was answered on May 14, 1948.

The biblical prophecies regarding the rebirth of Israel as a nation on May 14, 1948, the end of their tragic worldwide dispersion, and subsequent captivities show us that God has been involved in their history every step of the way. Specifically, Christianity is not based on blind and theoretical faith, but is based on facts and evidences that could be verified in specific ways.

CHAPTER SIXTEEN

APPROACHING THE FINAL STAGE

History, as it is explained from the biblical standpoint, began with divine purposeful creation and its final consummation will be with Christ's second coming. If we were to examine past world events and analyze their trends, there is strong evidence that the world is moving toward the final stage for Christ's return. Biblical materials provide us with signs that lead up to the final stage.

Setting the Ultimate Stage for the End

A great number of Christians believe Israelites return to the Promised Land as one of the most contributing evidence for the signal of the final stage of the end (Ezek. 37:4–13; Matt. 24:29–35). What is problematic in using fulfilled prophecies to exactly gauge the end times is that it is very difficult to determine how close our present time is to that described using the prophesized events. Jesus said, "No one knows about that day or hour," (Matt. 24:36) that Christ will return as the ". . . Lord will come like a thief in the night" (2 Pet. 3:10). However, the current global struggles and emerging trends point to the close possibility and similarities of the chain of world events prophesied in the Bible for setting the final stage of the end.

When Will it All End?

Many people do not hesitate to say that we are living in the end times, an era during which the world will be plunged into a series of unimaginably upheaval wars. People want to know "when this will be happen?" and "what the sign of Christ's return and of the end of the age will be?" These questions about the end of the age and Christ's return are not new issues. Even Christ's own disciples raised such questions themselves, shortly before Christ's crucifixion.

Our holy Bible clearly delineates that no one but God knows the exact hour of the end. However, it alludes to the period of the end of times beginning with Christ's entry to the world (Acts 2:17) and His second return marking the end (Matt. 24:30; Acts 1:11). We can find more vivid signs occurring in the end times throughout the Bible. Christ disclosed the signs of His return and the end of the age to His disciples (Matt. 24–25; Luke 21:25). His disclosure included a prediction of the imminent destruction of Jerusalem and also pointed to the far distant future when the "times of gentiles" would come to an end of the age,

The Old Testament prophet, Zechariah, portrayed "the Day of the Lord" as a time when all the nations will gather together against the holy city of Jerusalem, and the Lord will go forth to protect Jerusalem and on that day His feet will stand on the Mount Olives, east of Jerusalem (Zech. 14:4). In addition, Peter, John, and Paul, state that one of the very last signs of the end times would be the appearance of the Antichrist—the most evil man in history—during the last days and that he would take hold of the absolute power throughout the world.

The Antichrist (so-called the Beast) will claim himself to be "god" on earth and his co-worker, the False Prophet, will demand that everyone worship him and his image, and force all of humanity to receive his mark, the Beast, 666, a universal human control system on their forehead or hand (Rev. 13:14–18). The prophetic calendar described in the Bible provides us with clues of events to occur that will lead up to the end of times. Current events and trends as they have occurred support that we may be drawing near the end.

Prophetic Calendar

- The spread of Christianity to all nations (Matt. 16:18).
- Israel's return to the Promised Land. This prophecy was fulfilled when Israel was established as an independent nation on May 14, 1948, marking its first time as a unified nation in two thousand years.
- The growth of the church (Matt. 13:31–32).
- Wars and rumors of wars (Joel 3:9–10).
- As described by Paul, the end will be filled with ". . . terrible times in the last days" (2 Tim. 3:1); filled with lovers of themselves, lovers of money, the unholy, the ungrateful, the treacherous and the rash, lovers of pleasure rather than lovers of God (2 Tim. 3:2–5).
- Appearance of false prophets (Matt. 24:4–24; 2 Pet. 2:1–3) with followers of deceiving spirits and demons (1 Tim. 4:1).
- Conflicts directed at Jerusalem in the Middle East (Ezek. 38:14–16; Zech. 12:2–3; Luke 21:20–22).
- An organized global economy (Rev. 13:16–17; Rev. 18:3–13).
- Formidable natural disasters (Matt. 24:7; Rev. 8:8–12; Rev. 16:2–8).

- Organization of a world government (Dan. 7:23; Rev. 13:8; Rev. 17:1–18).
- Appearance of the Antichrist (2 Thess. 2:3–8; 1 John 2:22; Rev. 13:1–18; Rom. 11:4).
- Tribulations (Dan. 12:1; Zeph. 1:14–18; 1 Thess. 5:1–3; Jer. 30:7).
- Repentance of Israel (Ezek. 39:7–8; Zech. 12:10; Rom. 11:1–27).
- Disappearance of Christians (Matt. 25:6; 1 Cor. 51–52; 2 Cor. 11:2; 1 Thess. 4:15–17).
- Battle of Armageddon (Isa. 24:1–6; Isa. 34:2–3; Zech. 13:8; Zech. 14:12–13).
- Victorious second coming of Christ (Matt. 24:30; Luke 21:25–28; Zech. 14:3–4; Rev. 9:11–16).

The end of times as prophesied in the Bible is near. As evidenced since creation and the history of man, it is clear that God continues to govern and rule in the affairs of man based upon His eternal plan and will. The created world provides abundant evidences for our understanding of both the "being" of the Creator, God and of His "ruling" by His ways. Without God, the Creator, we can make no sense of the world in which we live, and our existence would be meaningless. In my own view, I exist because the Creator, God of the universe and life wants me to be and the whole universe exists for a similar purpose.

Therefore, what has occurred in history and will occur is certainly no accident. We have been presented with clear signs of the existence of God and his involvement in our lives. We have our free will to choose or deny Him. If we do choose Him, then we can proclaim with Paul, "For in Him we live and move and have our being" (Acts 17:28), and our whole spirit, soul and body should be kept blameless at the coming of our Lord Jesus Christ (1 Thess. 5:23).

CHAPTER SEVENTEEN

THE QUESTION OF SUFFERING

After dealing with the difficult topic of the Holocaust in the previous chapter, you may be wondering why innocent people suffer. Some consider suffering to be God's punishment, and some think of it as a warning sign of what might lie ahead. Can God be "good" and still allow suffering?

The Atheistic View

The atheist says that if God creates everything, and if everything He creates is good, then He must be the cause of suffering. But they don't even buy that. They see the argument as being inconsistent with who God might be, if He actually existed (from their point of view). Instead they view suffering as chance. It happens as a consequence of the evolutionary process; it is survival of the fittest.

The Christian View

The Christian worldview says that the fundamental source of suffering is the direct result of disobedience to God. The Bible speaks of the origins of bad things. It speaks of a creation that is cursed because of people's violations of God's law (Gen. 3:17–18). It says that the entire creation has been groaning as in the pains of childbirth right up to the present time (Rom. 8:21–22).

According to these statements, our wrongful behaviors will have destructive consequences that are passed on to the rest of creation. We can see that in the sin of Adam. Paul reiterated that fact when he said, "Therefore, just as sin entered the world through one man, and death through sin, and in this way death came to all men, because all sinned" (Rom. 5:12).

Suffering can also be a test of our faith. Just look at Job's life. He was a righteous man who lost everything through no volition of his own. Satan asked to sift Job and God gave him permission. In a sense, Job suffered for his faith, which makes his suffering a privilege.

Other Causes

Not all suffering comes directly from God. The Creator is, in some sense, fundamentally limited in what He can and cannot do in His creation. Look at the earth moving around the sun regularly. The laws of nature are precise, highly reliable, and always work the same way. So gravity is the result of some suffering. We fall off ladders and items fall off buildings. The laws of nature treat everybody the same.

Sometimes suffering is caused by the carelessness of people. Airplanes crash. So do automobiles. All calamities have their own reasons, but we can't always know or understand what those reasons are.

Nobody likes pain, but it is not always bad. Pain in our bodies can be a sign that something is wrong. When we touch something hot, we feel pain in order to make us jerk our hand away before we are seriously burned. If we could not feel pain, our lives would be faced with many dangerous moments. So, in some cases, we should see pain as a positive.

Ludwig Van Beethoven grew up with an alcoholic father. His family was poor. He went to work at eleven years of age. His mother died when he was seventeen. When he was thirty, he lost his hearing—an extremely difficult sense to lose, given that he was a classical composer and pianist. He was in despair, but he did not lose his passion for music. He kept studying and was able to compose his famous ninth symphony. He found great meaning in his suffering. His greatness came not from good conditions but from making the best of "bad" conditions.

This means that attitude during times of suffering is very important. There is unknown truth in suffering: We can learn from it. Suffering brings patience, and through it an unspeakable treasure often appears before us. God gives us strength, patience, and hope as He renews our spiritual resources when we run dry. Suffering isn't incompatible with the character of a loving God, but God can and does achieve His purposes through painful suffering. Suffering restraints us, keeps us from committing evil, makes us humble, reminds us of our weaknesses, and drives us to God. He promises that all things will work together for good for those who love Him and are called according to His purpose (Rom. 8:28).